Table of Contents

D1405525

Welcome to the
World Famous San Diego Zoo!

Established in 1916 by Dr. Harry M. Wegeforth, the San Diego Zoo began with a small collection of animals left over from San Diego's 1915-1916 Panama-California International Exposition in Balboa Park. One day, Dr. Wegeforth heard the roaring of the lions at the Exposition and said to his brother "Wouldn't it be splendid if San Diego had a zoo! You know…I think I'll start one." And so he did. Nearly a century later, the San Diego Zoo is one of the most respected and well-known zoos in the world.

Today, the Zoo is home to more than 4,500 mammals, birds, reptiles, and amphibians and a world-class botanical garden as well. The gardens are an important research and educational resource for scientists and students from around the world, and include nearly 100 endangered and threatened species and varieties of plants.

All of the San Diego Zoo's profits from admission fees as well as food and souvenir sales go back to support the work of the Zoological Society of San Diego. The Society is dedicated to the conservation of endangered species and their habitats, and engages in conservation and research work around the world. The Zoological Society of San Diego contributes greatly to research and preservation efforts around the globe, realizing that in working together, we stand a better chance of bringing the importance and beauty of the wild world back into focus.

Monkey Trails and Forest Tales

Joan B. Kroc's Monkey Trails and Forest Tales habitat is the naturalistic home to more than 30 species of African and Asian birds, mammals, reptiles, and amphibians, some of the world's most exotic and endangered wildlife. Here, you can enjoy an eye-to-eye view in the treetop canopy with some of the most rare and endangered monkeys on earth: Golden-bellied mangabeys, Schmidt's guenon, and mandrills. Or you can take the forest path and encounter exotic pigs. And be sure to look for the secretive and mysterious clouded leopard, lurking in the trees and shadows.

An African aviary is filled with exotic birds, and at the western end of Monkey Trails is an African riverbed habitat with aquatic tanks for watching underwater activities and behaviors of pygmy hippos and different species of crocodiles. Smaller exhibits house tortoises, tarantulas, scorpions, and more. And remember to check out the endangered plants as well—you'll see everything from a big ficus to African apricots to orchids and plumeria.

Tiger River

Tiger River is the San Diego Zoo's Asian rain forest bioclime, designed to instill you with a sense of wonder, discovery, and appreciation for the fragility of one of the world's most threatened environments. In Tiger River, you'll stroll along a riverbed pathway that leads to a tiger's lair, a crocodile pool and a fishing cat's den. The Malayan tiger habitat was designed to resemble their natural jungle home, and was built on a steep slope that gives the tigers plenty of exercise. A waterfall splashing into a pool and logs to climb on or use as scratching posts give the tigers a variety of things to do.

The marsh aviary is filled with birds such as storm and milky storks, imperial pigeons and white-collared kingfishers. Unusual Malayan tapirs, with their trunk-like snouts, like to lounge in their private pool. You may see fishing cats using their webbed paws to catch fish swimming in the stream that runs through their habitat. Nearby are freshwater crocodiles floating in their own special lake or sunbathing on their private beach.

Ituri Forest

Ituri Forest is one of the San Diego Zoo's most entertaining places to watch inter-species interactions. It is designed to give the visitor an easy-to-navigate rain forest experience. You can watch swamp monkeys frolic and see "eye-to-nostril" with our gregarious river hippos either from above water or below. The fish you see in the hippo pool are tilapia. They help keep the water clean by eating the hippos' dung and scraping away algae. They will even give the hippos a "massage" by scraping away old skin and growths.

Be sure to look for forest buffalos and okapis foraging in the forest as well. The forest buffalo looks like it has one long two-pointed horn planted on top of its head instead of two horns. The okapi can clean its own ears with its very long purple tongue!

What tall grass is used by more than half of the world's humans, grows faster than any other plant on Earth, and is said to have a thousand uses? It's bamboo! Look for bamboo growing in the Ituri Forest as well.

Gorilla Tropics

The key to Gorilla Tropics is the gorillas' habitat. With its natural land-scape of cascading waterfalls, open meadow, and climbing areas, Gorilla Tropics provides these vegetarian giants with a healthy living environment that adds to their wellbeing. Gorillas are members of a very complex social group, and the unique living habitat of Gorilla Tropics greatly helps to encourage their natural behavior.

Also in Gorilla Tropics, you'll find bonobos, also known as pygmy chimpanzees. What you'll also notice is that these intelligent animals are a lot of fun to watch. Across the path from the bonobos you'll find impressive crowned eagles. Their treetop perches are at eye level, which is a wonderful way to see these large birds of prey. Next door are Angolan colobus monkeys with their fringe of long white hair.

Scripps Aviary is a lush African rain forest complete with rushing waterfalls and exotic plants. Look up and you might spot some of the more than 200 colorful African native birds, or sit for a bit on one of the pathway benches. As you look around, you'll get a good feel from the flora and fauna you'd see in an African forest. Many of the plants in Gorilla Tropics are native to Africa, including the African tulip tree, hibiscus, and giant bird-of-paradise.

Aviaries

One of the special treats of the Zoo is the opportunity to observe our feathered friends without any barriers. The walk-through aviaries offer a chance to get up-close and eye-to-eye with a wide variety of bird species as they occupy their own portion of forest, from treetop to ground level.

In Owens Rain Forest Aviary, you can enjoy a gentle trek along an elevated, winding pathway that stretches more than 1,000 feet (305 meters) in length. The path begins at treetop level and immerses you in a forest canopy amidst scores of brilliantly colored tropical birds. The sound of water splashing on rocks attracts your attention to a waterfall, cascading into a pond where exotic fish like tiger barbs and rainbow fish glide through the water. Thick glass panels form one side of the pond, making it easy for you to marvel at these colorful swimmers.

As you amble through Scripps Aviary in Gorilla Tropics, be sure to stop now and then to sit on the path-way benches. As you look around, you'll get a good feel for the flora and fauna you'd see in an African forest. The aviary even has waterfalls and gentle showers.

You'll notice that the trees and bush-es are not trimmed and groomed like the plants on Zoo grounds. There's a reason for that. Aviary plants are extremely important for encouraging natural avian behavior, whether the birds use them for marking territories, making nests, or as special perches for courtship displays.

Sun Bear Forest

In Sun Bear Forest, the upper canopy of a rain forest is formed by the spreading leaves and branches of palms and ficus trees. Ornamental bananas, beechey bamboo, and camphor trees create the mid-canopy, and a mix of ferns, shrubs, flowers, and ornamental grasses makes up the understory of the Asian-style rain forest.

Bornean sun bears, the smallest bears in the world, are one of the most enjoyable animals to observe, especially in the natural setting of Sun Bear Forest. Here, the sun bears, named for the golden crescents on their chests, display their playful nature. Extremely agile and often comical, sun bears are great tree climbers and make excellent use of their enclosure's climbing structures.

An Asian-themed aviary is home to fairy bluebirds and fruit doves. Other residents of Sun Bear Forest include Gabriella's crested gibbons, nocturnal binturongs (or bear cats), and lion-tailed macaques.

Sun Bear Forest has a spectacular collection of Asian plants, including a number of gingers, which are actually an extension of Fern Canyon's gingers. Many people don't realize there are more than 2,500 species of ginger.

Reptile House and Reptile Mesa

The Reptile House at the San Diego Zoo has delighted and awed visitors for generations. A stroll around its perimeter allows you to safely view an amazing collection of pythons, cobras, boas, tortoises, rattlesnakes, and gila monsters up close. To the west of the Reptile House, visitors can meander down Reptile Mesa, pausing to admire Cuban and Anegada rock iguanas. Some of the Zoo's oldest residents can be found here as well – the Galapagos tortoises. Many of our Galapagos tortoises have been with us since 1928, making them the oldest residents in the Zoo. They arrived here as adults and we estimate their age to be over 100 years old! Venture into the smaller Klauber Buildings on the edge of Reptile Mesa to view frogs, toads, salamanders, snake-necked turtles, and the bizarre-looking matamata.

Reptile Mesa also has all kinds of exotic-looking plants (including, appropriately, dragon trees) from all kinds of remote locations.

Giant Pandas

The San Diego Zoo has had a love affair with giant pandas ever since two of the black-and-white bears came to visit in 1987. In 1996, the Zoo's Giant Panda Research Station opened to house and study the giant panda in order to ensure its survival. Since then, three cubs have been born at the Zoo.

Giant pandas are about the size of a stick of butter at birth. They have no hair and are helpless. The mother panda takes great care of her cub, holding it close to her chest. She doesn't leave the cub or the den for the first several days after the cub is born.

Bamboo is the most important plant in a giant panda's life. Pandas live in cold and rainy bamboo forests high in the mountains of western China. They seem pretty quiet, but giant pandas can bleat, roar, growl, and honk. Pandas spend at least 12 hours each day eating bamboo. Pandas eat as much as 84 pounds (38 kilograms) of bamboo each day. Giant pandas have also been known to eat grasses, bulbs, fruits, some insects, and even rodents and carrion.

Polar Bear Plunge

This exhibit brings the summer Arctic tundra south to San Diego, with Siberian reindeer, Pallas' cats, northern birds, and native plants, along with polar bears. The focal point of the exhibit is, naturally, the Plunge. From the underwater viewing room you can see how agile and playful the polar bears really are. In fact, they're known to swim right up to the glass to check out all the humans on display! The polar bear's nose is so powerful it can smell a seal on the ice 20 miles (32 kilometers) away, sniff out a seal's den that has been covered with snow, and even find a seal's air hole in the ice up to one mile (1.6 kilometers) away. With this ability, it's easy to understand their nickname: "Noses with legs."

Some of the most popular animals in Polar Bear Plunge are not big and white. They're not even furry. These crowd pleasers are diving ducks, such as buffleheads, smews, and eiders, housed in the aviary with the chilled pond and the underwater viewing window.

Horns and Hooves

The Zoo has several varieties of hoofed creatures, including giraffes, zebras, antelopes, gazelles, pigs, wild cattle, and takins. And how can you tell if you're looking at a goat or a sheep? If a male has the familiar beard, or goatee, then he's probably a goat; male sheep don't have beards. Another hint is the horns: a male sheep's horns usually curl and a goat's are straight. But, of course, there are exceptions. Both male and female goats and sheep have horns, but those of the males are much larger. The horns are made of keratin, like our fingernails, and they are permanent, growing throughout the animal's lifetime. A growth ring is deposited each winter. By counting those rings, it's possible to tell the animal's age. In contrast, deer antlers are made of bone and are shed and regrown every year. You'll also see a variety of adaptations to nature in the zebras' stripes, the giraffes' spots, the gazelles' ability to pronk, the eland's leaps and more.

Children's Zoo

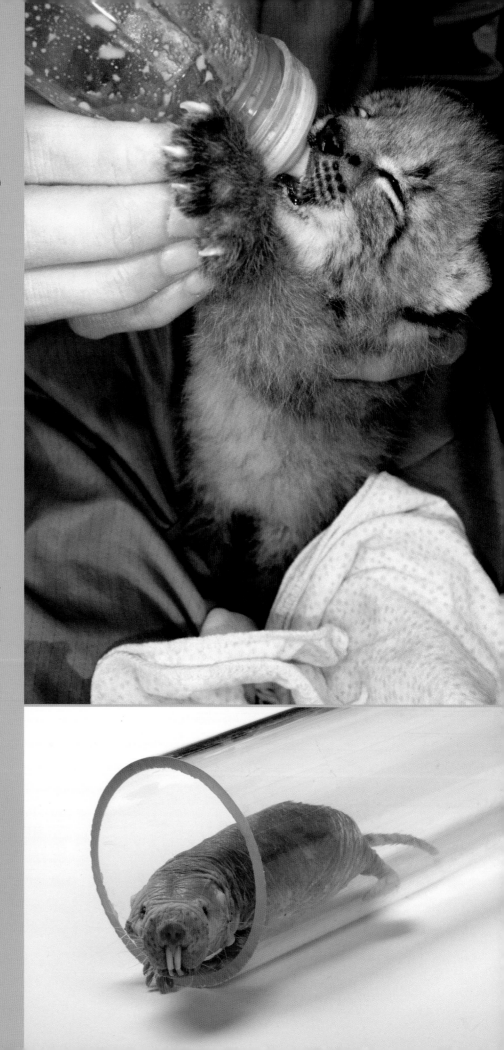

The Children's Zoo has more than 30 special animal exhibits and activities designed with our younger visitors in mind. The popular Petting Paddock allows kids a chance to feel the woolly coat of a sheep or comb a gentle goat's hair. The animal nursery has large viewing windows to let you watch animal babies being bottle-fed or cuddled by caring keepers. The Children's Zoo has animals not found anywhere else on Zoo grounds, such as wombats, spider monkeys and the ever-fascinating naked mole rats. Bugtown— The Itty-Bitty City explores the wonders of insects and other invertebrates, exhibiting each species in a miniature version of its natural habitat. You'll see giant water bugs, diving beetles, scorpions, tarantulas, katydids, and praying mantises. Each spring you can watch honeybees in their glass-lined hive. The Children's Zoo also has a variety of gardens that are both educational and functional: My Color Garden has plants grouped according to color; the Butterfly and Backyard Habitat gardens have plants to attract butterflies, birds, and other wildlife; Wig L. Worm's Composting Garden shows how easy it is to turn garbage into garden mulch with the help of earthworms.

During the summer, weekends, and other seasonal holidays, the Children's Zoo also offers shows, including presentations by our wacky resident scientist, Dr. Zoolittle, who delights audiences with his zany science shows. At various times of the year the Children's Zoo is host to special animal-themed events that include craft stations, up-close animal encounters, and more. And the famous racing pigeons are fun to watch as they fly overhead before returning to their Children's Zoo roost.

Shows

The San Diego Zoo's Sea Lion Show at Wegeforth Bowl

The Zoo's Sea Lion Show begins with a roar. It spotlights animals that can be found in national parks around the globe and, as always, features our charismatic California sea lions. You may even get to be part of the show!

The San Diego Zoo's Wild Ones Show at Hunte Amphitheater

The Wild Ones—Legends and Lore show delves into the legend and lore of both predators and prey from around the world. You'll witness the mystery of their natural behaviors. You may even get a chance to participate!

Welcome to the
San Diego Zoo's Wild Animal Park!

In 1969, the director of the Zoological Society of San Diego saw the need for a facility to breed endangered species in a naturalized habitat. His aim was to provide zoos with the animals they needed to ensure genetic diversity and protect endangered species from extinction. The Wild Animal Park was the creation of Dr. Charles Schroeder, Society director from 1954 to 1972. Dr. Schroeder had the foresight to realize that extinctions would accelerate unless zoos began conserving animals. He first envisioned the Wild Animal Park as a backcountry facility to breed animals for the San Diego Zoo and other zoos, creating self-sustaining animal populations.

The San Diego Zoo's Wild Animal Park is an expansive wildlife sanctuary that is home to more than 3,500 animals representing more than 400 species. Its renowned botanical collection represents 3,500 species and 1.5 million specimens. Over half of the Park's 1,800 acres (730-hectares) have been set aside as protected native species habitat.

"Join us here…to contemplate the wild animals of the world and nature's wilderness…to strengthen a commitment to wildlife conservation throughout the world, and to strive toward man's own survival through the preservation of nature." This official theme is truly embodied in the efforts of the Wild Animal Park staff, all who contribute to its success, and by the guests who visit here each year to enlarge their view of the possibilities for man and wilderness to live in harmony.

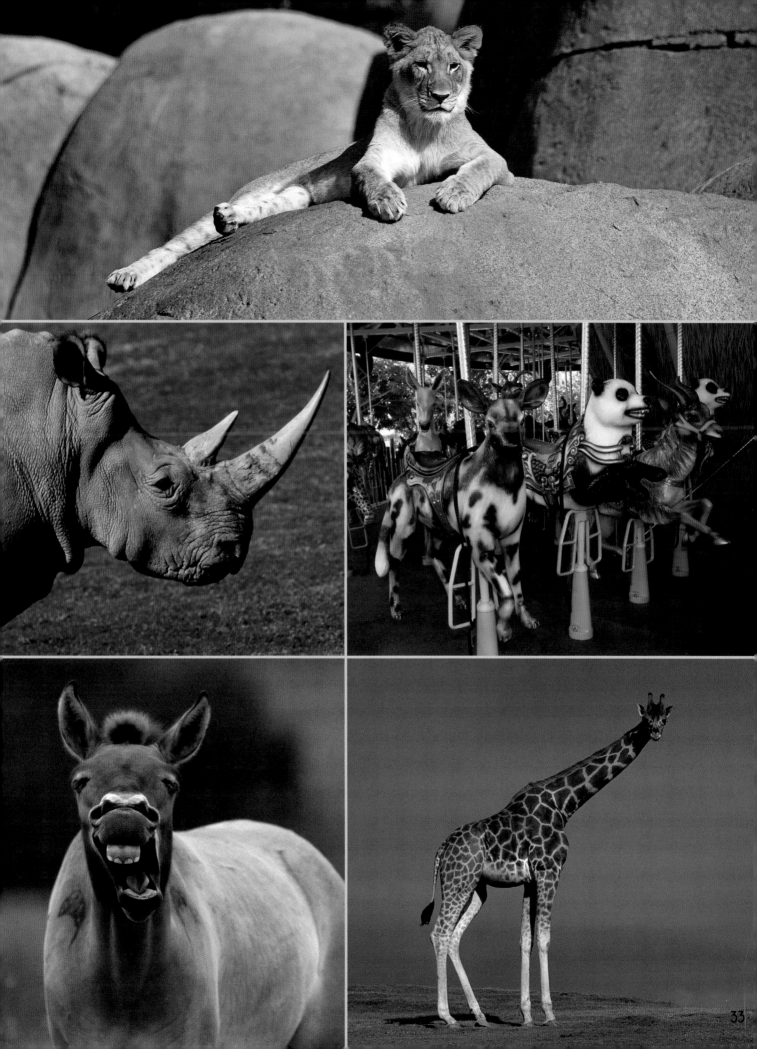

Nairobi Village

As you enter the Wild Animal Park, you'll find yourself in Nairobi Village, the bustling center of animal exhibits, shows, shops, restaurants and activities. In Nairobi Village, there are opportunities to interact with animals in the Petting Kraal and Animal Care Center, or one of the many shows available. There are also birds from many different parts of the world, found in the waterways of Nairobi Village or in one of the three aviaries or Condor Ridge. Nairobi Village is home to most of the smaller animals at the Wild Animal Park, with apes, lemurs, and insects. This is also your starting point for the Kilimanjaro Safari Walk or the Wgasa Bush Line Railway tour of the "wilder" portions of the park.

Almost all of the original plantings in Nairobi Village are from South and East Africa. Many of the African plants in Nairobi Village were grown from seed because full-grown plants were not available.

Hidden Jungle

A tropical rain forest is teeming with wildlife, beautiful but often hard to see. In the Hidden Jungle, a glass-walled greenhouse exhibit, you get a chance to observe the wonderful secrets of the rain forests, which are rapidly disappearing around the world. The Hidden Jungle's climate-controlled environment allows you to see some of the most delicate and fascinating creatures around, including neo-tropical birds and tropical plants. The dense growth and variety of plants provide important cover and food sources for Hidden Jungle residents. Extensive drip-irrigation and misting systems contribute to the tropical atmosphere, allowing orchids, bromeliads, and other epiphytes to grow. Look for exotic creatures such as quetzals, tanagers, honeycreepers, fruitcrows, stick insects, tarantulas and poison dart frogs.

In the spring, the Hidden Jungle gets an added dose of color during our annual Butterflies and Orchids event, when thousands of colorful butterflies hatch and add their gentle, fluttering presence to the wonders of this extraordinary exhibit. They adorn orchids, bromeliads, lantanas, and even our guests! When butterflies land on you or nearby, please enjoy them without touching—the butterflies' delicate wings are easily damaged by the oil on our fingers.

Heart of Africa

This is a magical journey that will transport you to the Heart of Africa, a safari—which means "travel" in Swahili—that takes you to Africa without the need of a passport! The heart and soul of Africa is its amazing diversity of species, which includes some of the most widely recognized and admired animals in the world. The Wild Animal Park has captured the enduring spirit of Africa's wild places in its Heart of Africa exhibit, bringing you close to such majestic animals as okapis, giraffes, warthogs, ground hornbills, and cheetahs. Opportunities for meeting animals face to face abound in the Heart of Africa. On most days you can watch a cheetah enjoy its afternoon meal while its keeper shares interesting facts about the fastest land mammal.

Trainers offer daily up-close Animal Encounters on the Heart of Africa lawn. And feeding shy, gentle giraffes can be the highlight of your day at the Heart of Africa's Giraffe Feeding station, where giraffe food is available for purchase, appetites permitting, of course!

Lion Camp

You're nose to nose with a lion, literally! Those big, golden eyes are staring at you with fixed and piercing intensity, the solid head and enormous paws more than hinting at the power of the animal you're facing. Is this it– are you lunch? No, you're just experiencing the amazing close encounters of Lion Camp: The Sylvia G. Straton Lion Savanna! There is a thick glass window between you and the lions, but when you're standing there and one comes charging up to the rocks only inches away, you might just forget that for a moment. Lion Camp is designed to bring you right into the world of African lions, and to bring them into yours, in all their golden glory.

Lions are the only cats that live in large, social groups, called "prides." A pride is made up of 3 to 30 lions. The pride consists of lionesses (mothers, sisters, and cousins), and their cubs, along with a few unrelated adult males. The pride has a close bond and is not likely to accept a stranger. The unrelated males stay a few months or a few years, but the older lionesses stay together for life. In dry areas with less food, prides are smaller, with two lionesses in charge. In habitats with more food and water, prides can have four to six adult lionesses. In addition to bringing lions and people together, Lion Camp is designed to tell the lion's story. You'll find information about the challenges that this species is facing in Africa and what you can all do to ensure the survival of this beautiful animal.

Giraffe feeding

Head to Heart of Africa's giraffe feeding station to watch a prehensile tongue grab a snack!

A giraffe's feet are the size of a dinner plate—12 inches across (30.5 centimeters). These amazing animals have the same number of vertebrae in their necks as we do, seven, but each one is just much bigger than ours! A giraffe's tongue is 18 to 20 inches (46 to 50 centimeters) long and blue-black. Some people think the color is to keep the tongue from getting sunburned. Different species of giraffes have different markings and colors. And would you believe the giraffe has the longest tail of any land mammal? They can be 8 feet (2.4 meters) long, including the tuft on the end! They also know how to use those long legs—the record running speed of a giraffe is 34.7 miles per hour (56 kilometers per hour). And while most of the time these genial giants are pretty quiet, giraffes can moo, hiss, roar, and whistle.

Kilimanjaro Safari Walk

The Kilimanjaro Safari Walk, named after the well-known mountain in Tanzania, Africa, takes you through some of the most scenic areas of the Wild Animal Park. There are a variety of possible routes, so take a look at your Park map and decide where you'd like to go. Spend the day exploring all the trails, or focus on one section. Depending on where you start, the path can lead you to the Park's vast botanical gardens, and/or past lions, tigers, or elephants. Plant life along the Safari Walk includes the Herb Garden, Protea Garden, Conifer Forest, Baja & Old World Succulents Gardens, Bonsai Pavilion, Epiphyllum House, and Nativescapes Garden.

A stop at Kilima Point along the trail will give you a shady and panoramic view of the 100-acre (40-hectare) East Africa field exhibit, where you'll see herds of giraffes, gazelles, and wildebeest stroll by. Whether you spend an hour in one area or an entire day creating your own safari, it's a whole new view!

Lorikeet Landing

Experience a rainbow on your shoulder in the Wild Animal Park's Lorikeet Landing aviary. When you walk through Lorikeet Landing you are transported to the rain forests of Australia and New Guinea, the natural habitat of the rainbow lorikeet. These beautiful, colorful birds are also known as brush-tongued parrots because their tongues are specially adapted to extract nectar and pollen from flowers. But in Lorikeet Landing, the birds don't have to put in as much effort because you lend a hand—literally—in feeding the lorikeets!

As you extend a small cup of special nectar toward the sky, the hungry lorikeets will land on your arms and hands to get to their feed. The birds have been specially trained to overcome their natural fear of humans, and they aren't shy when it comes to feeding—several birds at one time may even sit on your arm, or even your head and shoulders. Talk about an interactive experience!

Balloon Safari

Get a bird's-eye view of the entire Wild Animal Park on this unique airborne ride, modeled after the hot air balloon tours of the Serengeti. Located just west of Lion Camp, this quiet, tethered, helium-filled balloon can carry up to 30 people and rises up to 400 feet (121 meters), giving riders a panoramic view of lions, rhinos, giraffes, wildebeest, and gazelle, as well as the beautiful San Pasqual Valley. Tickets for Balloon Safari are available at either the main entrance or at the balloon site. Balloon Safari operates daily, and each launch will last approximately 15 minutes.

Frequent Flyers Bird Show

The Wild Animal Park's Frequent Flyers Bird Show at Benbough Amphitheater

You'll love the high-flying antics of our winged wonders as they show off their amazing avian skills.